IBADAH CREATIONS

PREFACE

As we embark on the sacred journey of Ramadan in the year 2024, it is with great pleasure and humility that I present this Ramadan Planner. This carefully curated guide aims to assist you in making the most of this blessed month, providing you with a comprehensive tool to enhance your spiritual experience. In the pages that follow, you will find a wealth of resources, including daily planners, hadith trackers, Ramadan duas, and informative content that seeks to deepen your understanding of this auspicious time.

Ramadan is not merely a month of fasting but a holistic opportunity for self-reflection, spiritual growth, and acts of kindness. This planner is designed to help you organize your days, track your fasts, and connect with the profound teachings of Islam. Each section has been thoughtfully crafted to serve as a companion throughout your Ramadan journey, offering practical guidance and inspiration.

May this Ramadan Planner be a source of support and motivation for you as you strive for personal and spiritual excellence during this sacred month. May it facilitate your commitment to fasting, prayer, and acts of charity, and may your efforts be richly rewarded by the mercy and blessings of Allah.

Acknowledgement

I extend my sincere gratitude to Allah, the Most Merciful and Compassionate, for granting me the opportunity to create this Ramadan Planner. I am deeply thankful for the wisdom and guidance found in the teachings of Islam, which have inspired and shaped the content of this planner.

I would like to express my heartfelt appreciation to my family and friends for their unwavering support and encouragement throughout the planning and creation of this guide. Your understanding and patience have been invaluable.

A special thank you goes to the scholars, educators, and community leaders whose teachings and insights have enriched the content of this planner. May Allah reward them abundantly for their dedication to spreading knowledge and fostering a deeper connection to our faith.

I also want to acknowledge the entire team involved in the production of this Ramadan Planner, from designers to editors, for their hard work and commitment to excellence.

Lastly, I extend my appreciation to every individual who chooses to embark on this Ramadan journey with the help of this planner. May it be a source of guidance, inspiration, and blessings for you and your loved ones.

May Allah accept our efforts and grant us a fulfilling and spiritually enriching Ramadan.

Ibadah Creations

Ramadan Planner

Dua when Sighting the New Moon

اَللّٰهُمَّ أَهِلَّهُ عَلَيْنَا بِالْيُمْنِ وَالْإِيمَانِ وَالسَّلَامَةِ وَالْإِسْلَامِ وَالتَّوْفِيقِ لِمَا تُحِبُّ وَتَرْضىٰ رَبِّي وَرَبُّكَ اللّٰهُ

Allaahumma ahillahu 'alainaa bil-amni wal-eemaani, was-salaamati wal-Islaami, wat-tawfeeqi limaa tuhibbu Rabbanaa wa tardhaa, Rabbunaa wa Rabbukallaahu.

"O Allah, let the crescent moon appear over us with security and Iman; with peace and Islam; and with ability, for us to practice such actions which you love. (O Moon) your creator and my creator is Allah."

Ramadan Fast Tracker

1	2	3	4	5	6
7	8	9	10	11	12
13	14	15	16	17	18
19	20	21	22	23	24
25	26	27	28	29	30

30 Days

Tarawih Challenge

Day 1   Day 2   Day 3   Day 4   Day 5   Day 6

Day 7   Day 8   Day 9   Day 10   Day 11   Day 12

Day 13   Day 14   Day 15   Day 16   Day 17   Day 18

Day 19   Day 20   Day 21   Day 22   Day 23   Day 24

Day 25   Day 26   Day 27   Day 28   Day 29   Day 30

May Allah Make it Easy

DUA FOR TARAWEEH

سُبْحَانَ ذِي الْمُلْكِ وَالْمَلَكُوتِ سُبْحَانَ ذِي الْعِزَّةِ وَ الْعَظَمَةِ وَالْهَيْبَةِ وَالْقُدْرَةِ وَالْكِبْرِيَاءِ وَالْجَبَرُوتِ سُبْحَانَ الْمَلِكِ الْحَيِّ الَّذِي لَا يَنَامُ وَ لَا يَمُوْتُ سُبُّوحُ قُدُّوسُ رَبُّنَا وَ رَبُّ الْمَلَائِكَةِ وَ الرُّوحِ اللَّهُمَّ أَجِرْنَا مِنَ النَّارِ يَا مُجِيْرُ يَا مُجِيْرُ يَا مُجِيْرُ

"SubHaana dhil-mulki wal-malakoot, subHaana dhil-'izzati wal-'azmati wal-haybati wal-qudrati wal-kibri-yaa 'i wal-jabaroot, subhaanal malikil Hayyil ladhi laa yanaamu wa laa yamoot, subbu- Hun quddusun rabbunaa wa rabbul-malaa 'ikati war-ruH, Allaahum- ma ajirnaa minan naar, yaa mujiru, yaa mujiru, yaa mujir"

"Glory be to the Owner of the Kingdom of the earth and the heavens. Glory be to He who commands Respect and Honour and Magnificence & Awe and Power and Greatness and Omnipotence. Glory be to the Sovereign, the Ever-living. Who does not sleep nor die. He is the Most Praised, the Most Holy, Our Lord and the Lord of all the Angels and the Spirit (Jibraeel A.S). O Allah! Save us from the Fire of Hell. O Protector! O Protector! O Protector!"   Al-Bukhari 7/158.

The Blessed Month of Ramadan

Ramadan, the ninth month of the Islamic calendar is the month during which Muslims around the world fast from dawn to sunset. Ramadan aims to purify the soul and bring the individual closer to Allah (SWT). It is a special month because it is the month in which Allah revealed the Quran.The Quran directs our attention to Allah and all that is beneficial in this world and the next.

"O you who have believed, decreed

upon you is fasting as it was decreed

upon those before you that you

may become righteous"

-- Surat Al-Baqarah 2:183

The Holy Quran makes it clear in the following passage that fasting is mandatory for all Muslims and that they must fast if they want to remain virtuous.

"...But to fast is best for you, if you only knew." -- Surat Al-Baqarah 2:184

Fasting teaches restraint; the ability to control worldly desires and spend time in prayer and meditation. Fasting is a noble act that is much beloved by Allah (SWT).

During Ramadan, there are many ways to earn good deeds and worship Allah, such as praying the 'taraweeh' at night, reading and learning the Quran, giving charity, giving meals to the poor to break their fast, having good manners with everyone, especially parents, learning and teaching others about Islam, and following Prophet Muhammed صلى الله عليه وسلم

The Blessed Month of Ramadan

The month of Ramadan in which was revealed the Quran, a guidance for mankind and clear proofs for the guidance and the criterion (between right and wrong). So whoever of you sights (the crescent on the first night of) the month (of Ramadan i.e. is present at his home), he must observe Saum (fasts) that month, and whoever is ill or on a journey, the same number [of days which one did not observe Saum (fasts) must be made up] from other days. Allah intends for you ease, and He does not want to make things difficult for you. (He wants that you) must complete the same number (of days), and that you must magnify Allah [i.e. to say Takbir (Allahu-Akbar; Allah is the Most Great) on seeing the crescent of the months of Ramadan and Shawwal] for having guided you so that you may be grateful to Him. --

Surat Al-Baqarah 2:185

SUHUR DUA
DUAS FOR STARTING THE FAST

اللَّهُمَّ أَصُوْمُ لَكَ فَاغْفِرْ لِي مَا قَدَّمْتُ وَمَا أَخَرْتُ

ALLAHUMMA ASUMU LAKA FAGH FIR-LI MA QAD-DAMTU WA-MA AKH-KHARTU

O Allah! I shall fast for Your sake, so forgive my future and past sins.

بِصَوْمِ غَدٍ نَوَيْتُ مِنْ شَهْرِ رَمَضَان

BI-SAWMI GHADIN NAWAIYTU MIN SHAHRI RAMADHAN

I intend to keep the fast for tomorrow in the month of Ramadhan.

IFTAR DUA

DUAS FOR BREAKING THE FAST

اللَّهُمَّ لَكَ صُمْتُ وَبِكَ آمَنْتُ وَعَلَى رِزْقِكَ أَفْطَرْتُ

ALLAHUMMA LAKA SUMTU WA BIKA AAMANTU WA 'ALA RIZQ-IKA AFTARTU

O Allah! I shall fast for Your sake, so forgive my future and past sins.

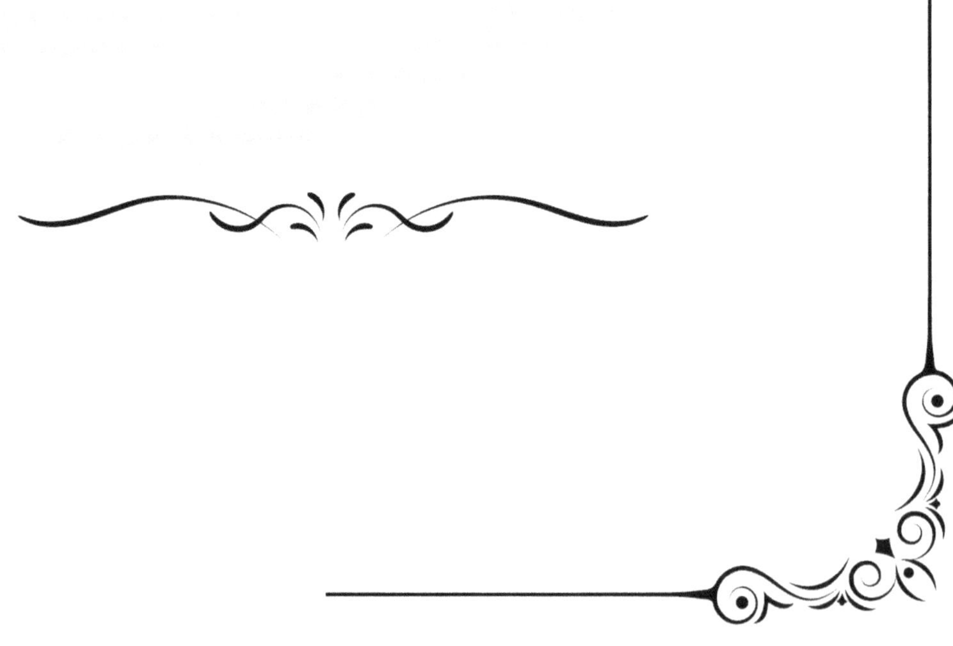

SPECIAL PRAYERS IN RAMADHAN

1st Ashra dua' (Days 1-10 of Mercy)

رَبِّ اغْفِرْ وَارْحَمْ وَأَنْتَ خَيْرُ الرَّحِمِينَ

> RABBIGH FIR WARHAM WA ANTA
>
> KHAIRUR RAAHIMEEN

O My Lord, forgive me, have mercy on me, you are the Most Merciful from those who give mercy.

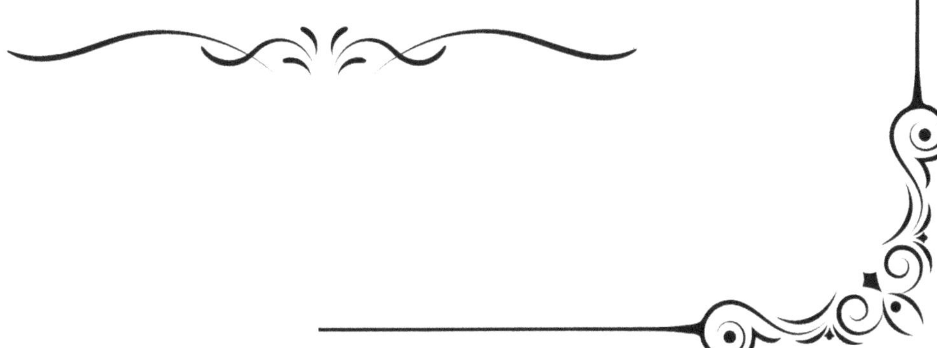

Ramadan Planner #1

Date

Sunday	Monday	Tuesday	Wednesday	Thursday	Friday	Saturday

DUA OF THE DAY

Ibadah Checklist

- ○ Fasting
- ○ Fajr
- ○ Dhuhr
- ○ Asr
- ○ Maghrib
- ○ Isha
- ○ Tarawih
- ○ Witr
- ○ Dhuha
- ○ Tahajud
- ○ Rawatib
- ○ Dhikr

Quote Verse of
the Day with
meaning

....

....

....

....

....

WATER

○ ○ ○ ○ ○ ○ ○ ○

What I'm Grateful for Today

DAILY CHECKLIST

○ Morning Adhkar	○ Istighfar
○ Evening Adhkar	○ Shukr
○ Deed Of The Day	○ Dhikr
○ Adhkar Before Sleep	○ Charity
○	○
○	○

DAILY TO DO LIST

- ○
- ○
- ○
- ○
- ○
- ○
- ○
- ○
- ○
- ○
- ○
- ○

Hadeeth Corner

الجنة تحت أقدام الأمهات

"Paradise lies under the feet of mothers."

(Sunan an-Nasa'i 3104, Musnad Ahmad 6651)

Serving parents is more
rewarding than voluntary Hajj

Ibn Abbas (RA) reported that a man came to the Prophet (ﷺ) and said:
"O Messenger of Allah! I want to go for Jihad, but my mother needs me."
The Prophet (ﷺ) replied:
"Stay with your mother, for Paradise is under her feet."

Ramadan Planner #2

Date

Sunday	Monday	Tuesday	Wednesday	Thursday	Friday	Saturday

DUA OF THE DAY

Ibadah Checklist

○ Fasting ○ Tarawih
○ Fajr ○ Witr
○ Dhuhr ○ Dhuha
○ Asr ○ Tahajud
○ Maghrib ○ Rawatib
○ Isha ○ Dhikr

Quote Verse of
the Day with
meaning

....
....
....
....
....

WATER

What I'm Grateful for Today

DAILY CHECKLIST

○	Morning Adhkar	○	Istighfar
○	Evening Adhkar	○	Shukr
○	Deed Of The Day	○	Dhikr
○	Adhkar Before Sleep	○	Charity
○		○	
○		○	

DAILY TO DO LIST

○
○
○
○
○
○
○
○
○
○
○
○

Hadeeth Corner

إِنَّمَا الْأَعْمَالُ بِالنِّيَّاتِ

"Actions are judged by intentions, and everyone will be rewarded according to what they intended."

(Sahih al-Bukhari 1, Sahih Muslim 1907)

Actions Are Judged by Intentions

A man once migrated to Madinah for the sake of a woman he wanted to marry.
The Prophet (ﷺ) said that his reward was only for what he intended—his migration was not for Allah, but for marriage.
This hadith teaches us to always purify our intentions.

Ramadan Planner #3

Date						
Sunday	Monday	Tuesday	Wednesday	Thursday	Friday	Saturday

DUA OF THE DAY

Ibadah Checklist

- ◯ Fasting
- ◯ Fajr
- ◯ Dhuhr
- ◯ Asr
- ◯ Maghrib
- ◯ Isha
- ◯ Tarawih
- ◯ Witr
- ◯ Dhuha
- ◯ Tahajud
- ◯ Rawatib
- ◯ Dhikr

Quote Verse of
the Day with
meaning

WATER

What I'm Grateful for Today

DAILY CHECKLIST

◯	Morning Adhkar	◯	Istighfar
◯	Evening Adhkar	◯	Shukr
◯	Deed Of The Day	◯	Dhikr
◯	Adhkar Before Sleep	◯	Charity
◯		◯	
◯		◯	

DAILY TO DO LIST

- ◯
- ◯
- ◯
- ◯
- ◯
- ◯
- ◯
- ◯
- ◯
- ◯
- ◯
- ◯

Hadeeth Corner

تَبَسُّمُكَ فِي وَجْهِ أَخِيكَ صَدَقَةٌ

"Smiling at your brother is an act of charity."

(Sunan at-Tirmidhi 1970, Sunan Ibn Majah 3257)

Smiling is Charity

A poor man once came to the Prophet (ﷺ) and said, "I have no wealth to give in charity."
The Prophet (ﷺ) replied, "Even a smile is charity!" This shows how small acts of kindness can earn great rewards.

Ramadan Planner #4

Date

Sunday	Monday	Tuesday	Wednesday	Thursday	Friday	Saturday

DUA OF THE DAY

Ibadah Checklist

- Fasting
- Fajr
- Dhuhr
- Asr
- Maghrib
- Isha
- Tarawih
- Witr
- Dhuha
- Tahajud
- Rawatib
- Dhikr

Quote Verse of
the Day with
meaning

DAILY CHECKLIST

○ Morning Adhkar		○ Istighfar	
○ Evening Adhkar		○ Shukr	
○ Deed Of The Day		○ Dhikr	
○ Adhkar Before Sleep		○ Charity	
○		○	
○		○	

DAILY TO DO LIST

WATER

What I'm Grateful for Today

Hadeeth Corner

خَيْرُ النَّاسِ أَنْفَعُهُمْ لِلنَّاسِ

"The best of people are those who bring the most benefit to others."

(al-Mu'jam al-Awsat)

The Best of People are Those Who Benefit Others

A companion once asked, "O Messenger of Allah, what is the best thing I can do?" The Prophet (ﷺ) replied, "Help others. Remove a difficulty from someone, guide someone, or even remove a harmful object from the road."

Ramadan Planner #5

Date

Sunday	Monday	Tuesday	Wednesday	Thursday	Friday	Saturday

DUA OF THE DAY

Ibadah Checklist

- ◯ Fasting
- ◯ Fajr
- ◯ Dhuhr
- ◯ Asr
- ◯ Maghrib
- ◯ Isha
- ◯ Tarawih
- ◯ Witr
- ◯ Dhuha
- ◯ Tahajud
- ◯ Rawatib
- ◯ Dhikr

Quote Verse of
the Day with
meaning

....

....

....

....

....

WATER

What I'm Grateful for Today

DAILY CHECKLIST

◯ Morning Adhkar	◯ Istighfar
◯ Evening Adhkar	◯ Shukr
◯ Deed Of The Day	◯ Dhikr
◯ Adhkar Before Sleep	◯ Charity
◯	◯
◯	◯

DAILY TO DO LIST

- ◯
- ◯
- ◯
- ◯
- ◯
- ◯
- ◯
- ◯
- ◯
- ◯
- ◯
- ◯

Hadeeth Corner

مَن لاَ يَرْحَمُ لاَ يُرْحَمُ

"He who is not merciful to others, will not be treated mercifully"

Sahih al-Bukhari 6013

The One Who is Merciful Will Receive Mercy

Abu Hurairah said; Al-Aqra' b. Habib saw that the Messenger of Allahﷺ was kissing Husain. He said: Abu Hurairah said; Al-Aqra b. Habib saw that the Messenger of Allahﷺ was kissing Husain. He said: I have ten children and I have never kissed any of them. The Messenger of Allahﷺ said: He who does not show tenderness will not be shown tenderness.

Ramadan Planner #6

Date

Sunday	Monday	Tuesday	Wednesday	Thursday	Friday	Saturday

DUA OF THE DAY

Ibadah Checklist

- ◯ Fasting
- ◯ Fajr
- ◯ Dhuhr
- ◯ Asr
- ◯ Maghrib
- ◯ Isha
- ◯ Tarawih
- ◯ Witr
- ◯ Dhuha
- ◯ Tahajud
- ◯ Rawatib
- ◯ Dhikr

Quote Verse of
the Day with
meaning

....
....
....
....
....

WATER

◊ ◊ ◊ ◊ ◊ ◊ ◊ ◊

What I'm Grateful for Today

DAILY CHECKLIST

◯ Morning Adhkar	◯ Istighfar
◯ Evening Adhkar	◯ Shukr
◯ Deed Of The Day	◯ Dhikr
◯ Adhkar Before Sleep	◯ Charity
◯	◯
◯	◯

DAILY TO DO LIST

- ◯
- ◯
- ◯
- ◯
- ◯
- ◯
- ◯
- ◯
- ◯
- ◯
- ◯
- ◯

Hadeeth Corner

مَنْ سَتَرَ مُسْلِمًا سَتَرَهُ اللَّهُ فِي الدُّنْيَا وَالآخِرَةِ

"Whoever covers the faults of a Muslim, Allah will cover his faults in this world and the Hereafter." (Sahih Muslim 2699)

Whoever Covers a Muslim's Faults, Allah Will Cover His Faults

Abu Hurairah (RA) reported that a man came to the Prophet (ﷺ) and said:
"O Messenger of Allah! My brother has committed a sin, should I expose him?"
The Prophet (ﷺ) replied:
"If you cover his fault, Allah will cover yours on the Day of Judgment."

Ramadan Planner #7

Date
Sunday	Monday	Tuesday	Wednesday	Thursday	Friday	Saturday

DUA OF THE DAY

Ibadah Checklist

- Fasting
- Fajr
- Dhuhr
- Asr
- Maghrib
- Isha
- Tarawih
- Witr
- Dhuha
- Tahajud
- Rawatib
- Dhikr

Quote Verse of
the Day with
meaning

WATER

What I'm Grateful for Today

DAILY CHECKLIST

○	Morning Adhkar	○	Istighfar
○	Evening Adhkar	○	Shukr
○	Deed Of The Day	○	Dhikr
○	Adhkar Before Sleep	○	Charity
○		○	
○		○	

DAILY TO DO LIST

Hadeeth Corner

لَيْسَ الشَّدِيدُ بِالصُّرَعَةِ، وَلَكِنَّ الشَّدِيدَ مَنْ يَمْلِكُ نَفْسَهُ عِنْدَ الْغَضَبِ

"The strong person is not the one who overcomes others, but the one who controls himself when angry."

(Sahih al-Bukhari 6114)

Controlling Anger is True Strength

Abu Hurairah (RA) reported that a man said to the Prophet (ﷺ):
"Advise me."
The Prophet (ﷺ) said: "Do not get angry."
The man repeated his question multiple times, and the Prophet (ﷺ) kept replying: "Do not get angry."

Ramadan Planner #8

Date

Sunday	Monday	Tuesday	Wednesday	Thursday	Friday	Saturday

DUA OF THE DAY

Ibadah Checklist

○ Fasting　　○ Tarawih
○ Fajr　　　 ○ Witr
○ Dhuhr　　 ○ Dhuha
○ Asr　　　　○ Tahajud
○ Maghrib　 ○ Rawatib
○ Isha　　　 ○ Dhikr

Quote Verse of
the Day with
meaning

DAILY CHECKLIST

○	Morning Adhkar	○	Istighfar
○	Evening Adhkar	○	Shukr
○	Deed Of The Day	○	Dhikr
○	Adhkar Before Sleep	○	Charity
○		○	
○		○	

DAILY TO DO LIST

WATER

What I'm Grateful for Today

Hadeeth Corner

إِنَ الصِّدْقَ يَهْدِي إِلَى الْبِرِّ، وَإِنَ الْبِرَّ يَهْدِي إِلَى الْجَنَّةِ

"Truthfulness leads to righteousness, and righteousness leads to Paradise."

(Sahih al-Bukhari 6094, Sahih Muslim 2607)

The Reward for Honesty

A young man came to the Prophet (ﷺ) and said, "O Messenger of Allah, I struggle with many sins. Please give me one piece of advice."
The Prophet (ﷺ) said, "Always speak the truth." The man followed this advice and soon abandoned his sinful ways.

Ramadan Planner #9

Date

Sunday	Monday	Tuesday	Wednesday	Thursday	Friday	Saturday

DUA OF THE DAY

Ibadah Checklist

- ◯ Fasting
- ◯ Fajr
- ◯ Dhuhr
- ◯ Asr
- ◯ Maghrib
- ◯ Isha

- ◯ Tarawih
- ◯ Witr
- ◯ Dhuha
- ◯ Tahajud
- ◯ Rawatib
- ◯ Dhikr

Quote Verse of
the Day with
meaning

....

....

....

....

....

WATER

What I'm Grateful for Today

DAILY CHECKLIST

◯	Morning Adhkar	◯	Istighfar
◯	Evening Adhkar	◯	Shukr
◯	Deed Of The Day	◯	Dhikr
◯	Adhkar Before Sleep	◯	Charity
◯		◯	
◯		◯	

DAILY TO DO LIST

- ◯
- ◯
- ◯
- ◯
- ◯
- ◯
- ◯
- ◯
- ◯
- ◯
- ◯
- ◯

Hadeeth Corner

مَن لَمْ يَشْكُرِ الْقَلِيلَ لَمْ يَشْكُرِ الْكَثِيرَ

"Whoever is not grateful for small things will
not be grateful for large things."

(Musnad Ahmad 18449)

Be Grateful for Small Blessings

A child thanked his mother for a small date.
The Prophet (ﷺ) smiled and said,
"Gratitude starts with small things."

Ramadan Planner #10

Date						
Sunday	Monday	Tuesday	Wednesday	Thursday	Friday	Saturday

DUA OF THE DAY

Ibadah Checklist

- ◯ Fasting
- ◯ Fajr
- ◯ Dhuhr
- ◯ Asr
- ◯ Maghrib
- ◯ Isha
- ◯ Tarawih
- ◯ Witr
- ◯ Dhuha
- ◯ Tahajud
- ◯ Rawatib
- ◯ Dhikr

Quote Verse of
the Day with
meaning

....
....
....
....
....

WATER

What I'm Grateful for Today

DAILY CHECKLIST

◯	Morning Adhkar	◯	Istighfar
◯	Evening Adhkar	◯	Shukr
◯	Deed Of The Day	◯	Dhikr
◯	Adhkar Before Sleep	◯	Charity
◯		◯	
◯		◯	

DAILY TO DO LIST

Hadeeth Corner

مَن نَفَّسَ عَن مُؤْمِنٍ كُرْبَةً نَفَّسَ اللَّهُ
عَنْهُ كُرْبَةً مِن كُرَبِ يَوْمِ الْقِيَامَةِ

"Whoever relieves a hardship of a believer,
Allah will relieve a hardship for him on the Day
of Judgment."   (Sahih Muslim 2699)

The One Who Removes Hardship, Allah Removes His Hardship

Once, a poor man was struggling to repay a loan. His creditor forgave the debt. The Prophet (ﷺ) said, "Allah will forgive this man just as he forgave his debtor."

Ramadan Planner #11

Date

Sunday	Monday	Tuesday	Wednesday	Thursday	Friday	Saturday

DUA OF THE DAY

Ibadah Checklist

- ◯ Fasting
- ◯ Fajr
- ◯ Dhuhr
- ◯ Asr
- ◯ Maghrib
- ◯ Isha
- ◯ Tarawih
- ◯ Witr
- ◯ Dhuha
- ◯ Tahajud
- ◯ Rawatib
- ◯ Dhikr

Quote Verse of
the Day with
meaning

DAILY CHECKLIST

◯	Morning Adhkar	◯	Istighfar
◯	Evening Adhkar	◯	Shukr
◯	Deed Of The Day	◯	Dhikr
◯	Adhkar Before Sleep	◯	Charity
◯		◯	
◯		◯	

DAILY TO DO LIST

WATER

What I'm Grateful for Today

Hadeeth Corner

طَلَبُ الْعِلْمِ فَرِيضَةٌ عَلَى كُلِّ مُسْلِمٍ

"Seeking knowledge is an obligation upon every Muslim."

(Sunan Ibn Majah 224)

Seeking Knowledge is an Obligation

A man once asked the Prophet (ﷺ), What if I die while seeking knowledge?" The Prophet (ﷺ) said, "Then you will die upon a path leading to Paradise."

Ramadan Planner #12

Date

Sunday	Monday	Tuesday	Wednesday	Thursday	Friday	Saturday

DUA OF THE DAY

Ibadah Checklist

- ○ Fasting
- ○ Fajr
- ○ Dhuhr
- ○ Asr
- ○ Maghrib
- ○ Isha
- ○ Tarawih
- ○ Witr
- ○ Dhuha
- ○ Tahajud
- ○ Rawatib
- ○ Dhikr

Quote Verse of
the Day with
meaning

WATER

What I'm Grateful for Today

DAILY CHECKLIST

○ Morning Adhkar	○ Istighfar
○ Evening Adhkar	○ Shukr
○ Deed Of The Day	○ Dhikr
○ Adhkar Before Sleep	○ Charity
○	○
○	○

DAILY TO DO LIST

- ○
- ○
- ○
- ○
- ○
- ○
- ○
- ○
- ○
- ○
- ○
- ○

Hadeeth Corner

أَحَبَّ أَسْمَائِكُمْ إِلَى اللَّهِ
عَبْدُ اللَّهِ وَعَبْدُ الرَّحْمَنِ

"The most beloved names to Allah are Abdullah and Abdur-Rahman."

(Sahih Muslim 2132)

The Best Names to Allah

When a man had a son, the Prophet (ﷺ) suggested the name Abdullah and said, "Allah loves this name."

Ramadan Planner #13

Date

Sunday	Monday	Tuesday	Wednesday	Thursday	Friday	Saturday

DUA OF THE DAY

Ibadah Checklist

- ○ Fasting
- ○ Fajr
- ○ Dhuhr
- ○ Asr
- ○ Maghrib
- ○ Isha
- ○ Tarawih
- ○ Witr
- ○ Dhuha
- ○ Tahajud
- ○ Rawatib
- ○ Dhikr

Quote Verse of
the Day with
meaning

DAILY CHECKLIST

○	Morning Adhkar	○	Istighfar
○	Evening Adhkar	○	Shukr
○	Deed Of The Day	○	Dhikr
○	Adhkar Before Sleep	○	Charity
○		○	
○		○	

DAILY TO DO LIST

- ○
- ○
- ○
- ○
- ○
- ○
- ○
- ○
- ○
- ○
- ○
- ○

WATER

What I'm Grateful for Today

Hadeeth Corner

إِيَّاكُمْ وَالْحَسَدَ فَإِنَّ الْحَسَدَ يَأْكُلُ الْحَسَنَاتِ كَمَا تَأْكُلُ النَّارُ الْحَطَبَ

"Avoid envy, for envy eats good deeds like fire consumes wood."

(Sunan Abu Dawood 4903)

Do Not Envy Others

Two brothers argued over wealth.
The Prophet (ﷺ) reminded them,
"Allah gives to whom He wills.
Do not let envy destroy your rewards."

Ramadan Planner #14

Date

Sunday	Monday	Tuesday	Wednesday	Thursday	Friday	Saturday

DUA OF THE DAY

Ibadah Checklist

○ Fasting   ○ Tarawih
○ Fajr   ○ Witr
○ Dhuhr   ○ Dhuha
○ Asr   ○ Tahajud
○ Maghrib   ○ Rawatib
○ Isha   ○ Dhikr

Quote Verse of
the Day with
meaning

....

....

....

....

....

WATER

What I'm Grateful for Today

DAILY CHECKLIST

○	Morning Adhkar	○	Istighfar
○	Evening Adhkar	○	Shukr
○	Deed Of The Day	○	Dhikr
○	Adhkar Before Sleep	○	Charity
○		○	
○		○	

DAILY TO DO LIST

○
○
○
○
○
○
○
○
○
○
○
○

Hadeeth Corner

لَا يُؤْمِنُ أَحَدُكُمْ حَتَّى يُحِبَّ لِأَخِيهِ مَا يُحِبُّ لِنَفْسِهِ

"None of you truly believes until he loves for his brother what he loves for himself."

(Sahih al-Bukhari 13)

Love for Your Brother What You Love for Yourself

A companion gave his last piece of bread to another.
The Prophet (ﷺ) said, "This is true faith!"

Ramadan Planner #15

Date

Sunday	Monday	Tuesday	Wednesday	Thursday	Friday	Saturday

DUA OF THE DAY

Ibadah Checklist

- ◯ Fasting
- ◯ Fajr
- ◯ Dhuhr
- ◯ Asr
- ◯ Maghrib
- ◯ Isha
- ◯ Tarawih
- ◯ Witr
- ◯ Dhuha
- ◯ Tahajud
- ◯ Rawatib
- ◯ Dhikr

Quote Verse of
the Day with
meaning

....

....

....

....

....

WATER

◌ ◌ ◌ ◌ ◌ ◌ ◌ ◌

What I'm Grateful for Today

DAILY CHECKLIST

◯	Morning Adhkar	◯	Istighfar
◯	Evening Adhkar	◯	Shukr
◯	Deed Of The Day	◯	Dhikr
◯	Adhkar Before Sleep	◯	Charity
◯		◯	
◯		◯	

DAILY TO DO LIST

- ◯
- ◯
- ◯
- ◯
- ◯
- ◯
- ◯
- ◯
- ◯
- ◯
- ◯
- ◯

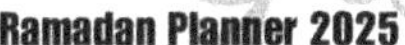

Hadeeth Corner

وَالصَّبْرُ ضِيَاءٌ

"Patience is light."

(Sahih Muslim 223)

Love for Your Brother What You
Love for Yourself

Anas ibn Malik (RA) reported that
the Prophet (ﷺ) said:
"When Allah loves a person, He tests
 them. Whoever is patient will have
great rewards."

Ramadan Planner #16

Date

Sunday	Monday	Tuesday	Wednesday	Thursday	Friday	Saturday

DUA OF THE DAY

Ibadah Checklist

- ○ Fasting
- ○ Fajr
- ○ Dhuhr
- ○ Asr
- ○ Maghrib
- ○ Isha
- ○ Tarawih
- ○ Witr
- ○ Dhuha
- ○ Tahajud
- ○ Rawatib
- ○ Dhikr

Quote Verse of
the Day with
meaning

WATER

What I'm Grateful for Today

DAILY CHECKLIST

○	Morning Adhkar	○	Istighfar
○	Evening Adhkar	○	Shukr
○	Deed Of The Day	○	Dhikr
○	Adhkar Before Sleep	○	Charity
○		○	
○		○	

DAILY TO DO LIST

- ○
- ○
- ○
- ○
- ○
- ○
- ○
- ○
- ○
- ○
- ○
- ○

Hadeeth Corner

مَا نَحَلَ وَالِدٌ وَلَدَهُ خَيْرًا مِنْ أَدَبٍ حَسَنٍ

"No father can give his child a better gift than good manners."

(Sunan at-Tirmidhi 4977)

The Best Gift to a Child is Good Manners

A father asked the Prophet (ﷺ) what he should teach his son. The Prophet (ﷺ) said, "Teach him good manners, for this is the best inheritance."

Ramadan Planner #17

Date						
Sunday	Monday	Tuesday	Wednesday	Thursday	Friday	Saturday

DUA OF THE DAY

Ibadah Checklist

- ○ Fasting
- ○ Fajr
- ○ Dhuhr
- ○ Asr
- ○ Maghrib
- ○ Isha
- ○ Tarawih
- ○ Witr
- ○ Dhuha
- ○ Tahajud
- ○ Rawatib
- ○ Dhikr

Quote Verse of
the Day with
meaning

....
....
....
....
....

WATER

What I'm Grateful for Today

DAILY CHECKLIST

○ Morning Adhkar	○ Istighfar
○ Evening Adhkar	○ Shukr
○ Deed Of The Day	○ Dhikr
○ Adhkar Before Sleep	○ Charity
○	○
○	○

DAILY TO DO LIST

- ○
- ○
- ○
- ○
- ○
- ○
- ○
- ○
- ○
- ○
- ○
- ○

Hadeeth Corner

لَا يَغْتَب بَعْضُكُمْ بَعْضًا

"Do not backbite one another."

(Quran 49:12)

Avoid Backbiting

A woman spoke ill of another. The Prophet (ﷺ) said, "You are eating the flesh of your sister!" She was shocked and repented.

Ramadan Planner #18

Date

Sunday	Monday	Tuesday	Wednesday	Thursday	Friday	Saturday

DUA OF THE DAY

Ibadah Checklist

- ○ Fasting
- ○ Fajr
- ○ Dhuhr
- ○ Asr
- ○ Maghrib
- ○ Isha
- ○ Tarawih
- ○ Witr
- ○ Dhuha
- ○ Tahajud
- ○ Rawatib
- ○ Dhikr

Quote Verse of
the Day with
meaning

....
....
....
....
....

WATER

What I'm Grateful for Today

DAILY CHECKLIST

○ Morning Adhkar	○ Istighfar
○ Evening Adhkar	○ Shukr
○ Deed Of The Day	○ Dhikr
○ Adhkar Before Sleep	○ Charity
○	○
○	○

DAILY TO DO LIST

- ○
- ○
- ○
- ○
- ○
- ○
- ○
- ○
- ○
- ○
- ○
- ○

Hadeeth Corner

وَإِمَاطَةُ الأَذَى عَنِ الطَّرِيقِ صَدَقَةٌ

"Removing something harmful from the road is
an act of charity."

(Sahih al-Bukhari 2989)

Removing Harm from the Road is Charity

A companion once saw a thorn on the
road and removed it.
The Prophet (ﷺ) said:
"Allah was pleased with him and
forgave his sins for that small act."

Ramadan Planner #19

Date						
Sunday	Monday	Tuesday	Wednesday	Thursday	Friday	Saturday

DUA OF THE DAY

Ibadah Checklist

- ◯ Fasting
- ◯ Fajr
- ◯ Dhuhr
- ◯ Asr
- ◯ Maghrib
- ◯ Isha
- ◯ Tarawih
- ◯ Witr
- ◯ Dhuha
- ◯ Tahajud
- ◯ Rawatib
- ◯ Dhikr

Quote Verse of
the Day with
meaning

....
....
....
....
....

WATER

◯ ◯ ◯ ◯ ◯ ◯ ◯ ◯

What I'm Grateful for Today

DAILY CHECKLIST

◯	Morning Adhkar	◯	Istighfar
◯	Evening Adhkar	◯	Shukr
◯	Deed Of The Day	◯	Dhikr
◯	Adhkar Before Sleep	◯	Charity
◯		◯	
◯		◯	

DAILY TO DO LIST

- ◯
- ◯
- ◯
- ◯
- ◯
- ◯
- ◯
- ◯
- ◯
- ◯
- ◯
- ◯

Hadeeth Corner

أَحَبُّ الأَعْمَالِ إِلَى اللَّهِ إِطْعَامُ الطَّعَامِ

"The most beloved deed to Allah is feeding the hungry."

(Musnad Ahmad 23408)

Feeding the Poor is a Path to Paradise

A man once asked the Prophet (ﷺ):
"What is the best way to earn Allah's love?"
The Prophet (ﷺ) replied:
"Feed the hungry, greet others with peace, and maintain family ties."

Ramadan Planner #20

Date						
Sunday	Monday	Tuesday	Wednesday	Thursday	Friday	Saturday

DUA OF THE DAY

Ibadah Checklist

- Fasting
- Fajr
- Dhuhr
- Asr
- Maghrib
- Isha
- Tarawih
- Witr
- Dhuha
- Tahajud
- Rawatib
- Dhikr

Quote Verse of
the Day with
meaning

DAILY CHECKLIST

Morning Adhkar	Istighfar
Evening Adhkar	Shukr
Deed Of The Day	Dhikr
Adhkar Before Sleep	Charity

DAILY TO DO LIST

WATER

What I'm Grateful for Today

Hadeeth Corner

دُعَاءُ الْمَرْءِ لِأَخِيهِ بِظَهْرِ الْغَيْبِ مُسْتَجَابٌ

"The supplication of a Muslim for his brother in his absence is accepted. The angel says: 'Ameen, and may you have the same.'"

(Sahih Muslim 2733)

Making Dua for Others Brings Angels' Prayers

Abu Darda (RA) reported that the Prophet (ﷺ) said:
"Whenever you pray for someone else, an angel prays for you in return."

Ramadan Planner #21

Date						
Sunday	Monday	Tuesday	Wednesday	Thursday	Friday	Saturday

DUA OF THE DAY

Ibadah Checklist

- ◯ Fasting
- ◯ Fajr
- ◯ Dhuhr
- ◯ Asr
- ◯ Maghrib
- ◯ Isha
- ◯ Tarawih
- ◯ Witr
- ◯ Dhuha
- ◯ Tahajud
- ◯ Rawatib
- ◯ Dhikr

Quote Verse of
the Day with
meaning

....
....
....
....
....

WATER

What I'm Grateful for Today

DAILY CHECKLIST

◯ Morning Adhkar	◯ Istighfar
◯ Evening Adhkar	◯ Shukr
◯ Deed Of The Day	◯ Dhikr
◯ Adhkar Before Sleep	◯ Charity
◯	◯
◯	◯

DAILY TO DO LIST

- ◯
- ◯
- ◯
- ◯
- ◯
- ◯
- ◯
- ◯
- ◯
- ◯
- ◯
- ◯

Hadeeth Corner

أَحَبُّ الْأَعْمَالِ إِلَى اللَّهِ أَدْوَمُهَا وَإِنْ قَلَّ

"The most beloved deeds to Allah are those that are done regularly, even if they are small."

(Sahih al-Bukhari 6464)

The Best Deeds Are Those Done Consistently

Aisha (RA) reported that the Prophet (ﷺ) would pray at night, and even when he became tired, he would still perform his prayers regularly. She asked him why, and he replied:
"Should I not be a grateful servant?"

Ramadan Planner #22

Date

Sunday	Monday	Tuesday	Wednesday	Thursday	Friday	Saturday

DUA OF THE DAY

Ibadah Checklist

○ Fasting ○ Tarawih

○ Fajr ○ Witr

○ Dhuhr ○ Dhuha

○ Asr ○ Tahajud

○ Maghrib ○ Rawatib

○ Isha ○ Dhikr

Quote Verse of
the Day with
meaning

....

....

....

....

....

WATER

What I'm Grateful for Today

DAILY CHECKLIST

○ Morning Adhkar	○ Istighfar
○ Evening Adhkar	○ Shukr
○ Deed Of The Day	○ Dhikr
○ Adhkar Before Sleep	○ Charity
○	○
○	○

DAILY TO DO LIST

○
○
○
○
○
○
○
○
○
○
○
○

Hadeeth Corner

وَاللَّهُ فِي عَوْنِ الْعَبْدِ مَا كَانَ الْعَبْدُ فِي عَوْنِ أَخِيهِ

"Allah helps a servant as long as the servant helps his brother."

(Sahih Muslim 2699)

Helping Others in Times of Need

Abu Hurairah (RA) reported that the Prophet (ﷺ) said:
"Whoever relieves a hardship for a believer, Allah will relieve a hardship for him on the Day of Judgment."

Ramadan Planner #23

Date

Sunday	Monday	Tuesday	Wednesday	Thursday	Friday	Saturday

DUA OF THE DAY

Ibadah Checklist

- ◯ Fasting
- ◯ Fajr
- ◯ Dhuhr
- ◯ Asr
- ◯ Maghrib
- ◯ Isha
- ◯ Tarawih
- ◯ Witr
- ◯ Dhuha
- ◯ Tahajud
- ◯ Rawatib
- ◯ Dhikr

Quote Verse of
the Day with
meaning

WATER

What I'm Grateful for Today

DAILY CHECKLIST

◯	Morning Adhkar	◯	Istighfar
◯	Evening Adhkar	◯	Shukr
◯	Deed Of The Day	◯	Dhikr
◯	Adhkar Before Sleep	◯	Charity
◯		◯	
◯		◯	

DAILY TO DO LIST

Hadeeth Corner

مَنْ دَلَّ عَلَى خَيْرٍ فَلَهُ مِثْلُ أَجْرِ فَاعِلِهِ

"Whoever guides someone to goodness will have a reward equal to the one who does it."

(Sahih Muslim 1893)

The One Who Guides Others to Good Gets the Same Reward

Abu Mas'ud (RA) reported that the Prophet (ﷺ) said:
"If you lead someone to do a good deed, you will share in the reward without reducing his reward."

Ramadan Planner #24

Date						
Sunday	Monday	Tuesday	Wednesday	Thursday	Friday	Saturday

DUA OF THE DAY

Ibadah Checklist

- ○ Fasting
- ○ Fajr
- ○ Dhuhr
- ○ Asr
- ○ Maghrib
- ○ Isha
- ○ Tarawih
- ○ Witr
- ○ Dhuha
- ○ Tahajud
- ○ Rawatib
- ○ Dhikr

Quote Verse of
the Day with
meaning

....
....
....
....
....

WATER

What I'm Grateful for Today

DAILY CHECKLIST

○ Morning Adhkar	○ Istighfar
○ Evening Adhkar	○ Shukr
○ Deed Of The Day	○ Dhikr
○ Adhkar Before Sleep	○ Charity
○	○
○	○

DAILY TO DO LIST

- ○
- ○
- ○
- ○
- ○
- ○
- ○
- ○
- ○
- ○
- ○
- ○

Hadeeth Corner

لَيْسَ الْغِنَى عَنْ كَثْرَةِ الْعَرَضِ،

وَلَكِنَّ الْغِنَى غِنَى النَّفْسِ

"Wealth is not having many possessions, but true wealth is being content in the heart."

(Sahih al-Bukhari 6446, Sahih Muslim 1051)

The Best Wealth is Contentment

Abu Hurairah (RA) reported that a man asked the Prophet (ﷺ):
"O Messenger of Allah, who is the richest?"
The Prophet (ﷺ) replied:
"The one who is content with what Allah has given him."

Ramadan Planner #25

Date

Sunday	Monday	Tuesday	Wednesday	Thursday	Friday	Saturday

DUA OF THE DAY

Ibadah Checklist

○ Fasting   ○ Tarawih
○ Fajr   ○ Witr
○ Dhuhr   ○ Dhuha
○ Asr   ○ Tahajud
○ Maghrib   ○ Rawatib
○ Isha   ○ Dhikr

Quote Verse of
the Day with
meaning

....

....

....

....

....

WATER

What I'm Grateful for Today

DAILY CHECKLIST

○ Morning Adhkar	○ Istighfar
○ Evening Adhkar	○ Shukr
○ Deed Of The Day	○ Dhikr
○ Adhkar Before Sleep	○ Charity
○	○
○	○

DAILY TO DO LIST

○
○
○
○
○
○
○
○
○
○
○
○

Hadeeth Corner

مَن يَلِي مِن هَذِهِ الْبَنَاتِ شَيئًا فَأَحْسَنَ إِلَيْهِنَّ كُنَّ لَهُ سِتْرًا مِنَ النَّارِ

"Whoever is in charge of (put to test by) these daughters and treats them generously, then they will act as a shield for him from the (Hell) Fire".

(Sahih Muslim 2733)

The Love Between Believers

Narrated 'Aisha: (the wife of the Prophet) A lady along with her two daughters came to me asking me (for some alms), but she found nothing with me except one date which I gave to her and she divided it between her two daughters, and then she got up and went away. Then the Prophet ﷺ came in and I informed him about this storye".

Ramadan Planner #26

Date

Sunday	Monday	Tuesday	Wednesday	Thursday	Friday	Saturday

DUA OF THE DAY

Ibadah Checklist

- ○ Fasting
- ○ Fajr
- ○ Dhuhr
- ○ Asr
- ○ Maghrib
- ○ Isha

- ○ Tarawih
- ○ Witr
- ○ Dhuha
- ○ Tahajud
- ○ Rawatib
- ○ Dhikr

Quote Verse of
the Day with
meaning

....

....

....

....

....

WATER

What I'm Grateful for Today

DAILY CHECKLIST

○	Morning Adhkar	○	Istighfar
○	Evening Adhkar	○	Shukr
○	Deed Of The Day	○	Dhikr
○	Adhkar Before Sleep	○	Charity
○		○	
○		○	

DAILY TO DO LIST

- ○
- ○
- ○
- ○
- ○
- ○
- ○
- ○
- ○
- ○
- ○
- ○

Hadeeth Corner

دُعَاءُ الْمَرْءِ لِأَخِيهِ بِظَهْرِ الْغَيْبِ مُسْتَجَابٌ

"The supplication of a Muslim for his brother in his absence is accepted. The angel says: 'Ameen, and may you have the same.'"

(Sahih Muslim 2733)

Making Dua for Others Brings Angels' Prayers

Abu Darda (RA) reported that the Prophet (ﷺ) said:
"Whenever you pray for someone else, an angel prays for you in return."

Ramadan Planner #27

Date

Sunday	Monday	Tuesday	Wednesday	Thursday	Friday	Saturday

DUA OF THE DAY

Ibadah Checklist

- Fasting
- Fajr
- Dhuhr
- Asr
- Maghrib
- Isha
- Tarawih
- Witr
- Dhuha
- Tahajud
- Rawatib
- Dhikr

Quote Verse of
the Day with
meaning

WATER

What I'm Grateful for Today

DAILY CHECKLIST

Morning Adhkar	Istighfar
Evening Adhkar	Shukr
Deed Of The Day	Dhikr
Adhkar Before Sleep	Charity

DAILY TO DO LIST

Hadeeth Corner

دُعَاءُ الْمَرْءِ لِأَخِيهِ بِظَهْرِ الْغَيْبِ مُسْتَجَابٌ

"The supplication of a Muslim for his brother in his absence is accepted. The angel says: 'Ameen, and may you have the same.'"

(Sahih Muslim 2733)

Making Dua for Others Brings Angels' Prayers

Abu Darda (RA) reported that the Prophet (ﷺ) said:
"Whenever you pray for someone else, an angel prays for you in return."

Ramadan Planner #28

| Date | | | | | | |
| Sunday | Monday | Tuesday | Wednesday | Thursday | Friday | Saturday |

DUA OF THE DAY

Ibadah Checklist

- ⭘ Fasting
- ⭘ Fajr
- ⭘ Dhuhr
- ⭘ Asr
- ⭘ Maghrib
- ⭘ Isha
- ⭘ Tarawih
- ⭘ Witr
- ⭘ Dhuha
- ⭘ Tahajud
- ⭘ Rawatib
- ⭘ Dhikr

Quote Verse of
the Day with
meaning

WATER

What I'm Grateful for Today

DAILY CHECKLIST

⭘ Morning Adhkar	⭘ Istighfar
⭘ Evening Adhkar	⭘ Shukr
⭘ Deed Of The Day	⭘ Dhikr
⭘ Adhkar Before Sleep	⭘ Charity
⭘	⭘
⭘	⭘

DAILY TO DO LIST

Hadeeth Corner

دُعَاءُ الْمَرْءِ لِأَخِيهِ بِظَهْرِ الْغَيْبِ مُسْتَجَابٌ

"The supplication of a Muslim for his brother in his absence is accepted. The angel says: 'Ameen, and may you have the same.'"

(Sahih Muslim 2733)

Making Dua for Others Brings Angels' Prayers

Abu Darda (RA) reported that the Prophet (ﷺ) said:
"Whenever you pray for someone else, an angel prays for you in return."

Ramadan Planner #29

Date

Sunday	Monday	Tuesday	Wednesday	Thursday	Friday	Saturday

DUA OF THE DAY

Ibadah Checklist

- ○ Fasting
- ○ Fajr
- ○ Dhuhr
- ○ Asr
- ○ Maghrib
- ○ Isha

- ○ Tarawih
- ○ Witr
- ○ Dhuha
- ○ Tahajud
- ○ Rawatib
- ○ Dhikr

Quote Verse of
the Day with
meaning

DAILY CHECKLIST

○ Morning Adhkar	○ Istighfar
○ Evening Adhkar	○ Shukr
○ Deed Of The Day	○ Dhikr
○ Adhkar Before Sleep	○ Charity
○	○
○	○

DAILY TO DO LIST

- ○
- ○
- ○
- ○
- ○
- ○
- ○
- ○
- ○
- ○
- ○
- ○
- ○

WATER

What I'm Grateful for Today

Hadeeth Corner

دُعَاءُ الْمَرْءِ لِأَخِيهِ بِظَهْرِ الْغَيْبِ مُسْتَجَابٌ

"The supplication of a Muslim for his brother in his absence is accepted. The angel says: 'Ameen, and may you have the same.'"

(Sahih Muslim 2733)

Making Dua for Others Brings
Angels' Prayers

Abu Darda (RA) reported that the Prophet (ﷺ) said:
"Whenever you pray for someone else, an angel prays for you in return."

Ramadan Planner #30

Date

| Sunday | Monday | Tuesday | Wednesday | Thursday | Friday | Saturday |

DUA OF THE DAY

Ibadah Checklist

- ○ Fasting
- ○ Fajr
- ○ Dhuhr
- ○ Asr
- ○ Maghrib
- ○ Isha

- ○ Tarawih
- ○ Witr
- ○ Dhuha
- ○ Tahajud
- ○ Rawatib
- ○ Dhikr

Quote Verse of
the Day with
meaning

DAILY CHECKLIST

○ Morning Adhkar	○ Istighfar
○ Evening Adhkar	○ Shukr
○ Deed Of The Day	○ Dhikr
○ Adhkar Before Sleep	○ Charity
○	○
○	○

DAILY TO DO LIST

WATER

What I'm Grateful for Today

Hadeeth Corner

دُعَاءُ الْمَرْءِ لِأَخِيهِ بِظَهْرِ الْغَيْبِ مُسْتَجَابٌ

"The supplication of a Muslim for his brother in his absence is accepted. The angel says: 'Ameen, and may you have the same.'"

(Sahih Muslim 2733)

Making Dua for Others Brings Angels' Prayers

Abu Darda (RA) reported that the Prophet (ﷺ) said:
"Whenever you pray for someone else, an angel prays for you in return."

RAMADAN DUAS

اللَّهُمَّ أَجِرْنِي مِنَ النَّارِ

O Allah! I seek your protection from the hellfire (Abu Dawud)

اللَّهُمَّ إِنَّكَ عَفُوٌّ تُحِبُّ الْعَفْوَ فَاعْفُ عَنِّي

O Allah! You are most forgiving, you love to forgive, so forgive me (Tirmidhi)

RAMADAN DUAS

اللَّهُمَّ إِنِّي أَعُوذُ بِكَ مِنَ الْهَمِّ وَالْحَزَنِ، وَالْعَجْزِ وَالْكَسَلِ، وَالْبُخْلِ وَالْجُبْنِ، وَضَلَعِ الدَّيْنِ وَغَلَبَةِ الرِّجَالِ

ALLĀHUMMA INNĪ A`ŪDHU BIKA MINA 'L-ḥAMMI

WA 'L-ḥAZAN,

WA 'L-`AJZI WA 'L-KASAL,

WA 'L-BUKHLI WA 'L-JUBN,

WA ḍALA`ID-DAYNI WA GHALABATIR-RIJĀL.

O Allah! I seek refuge with You from worry and grief, from incapacity and laziness, from cowardice and miserliness, from being heavily in debt and from being overpowered by (other) men.

Al–Bukhari 7/158.

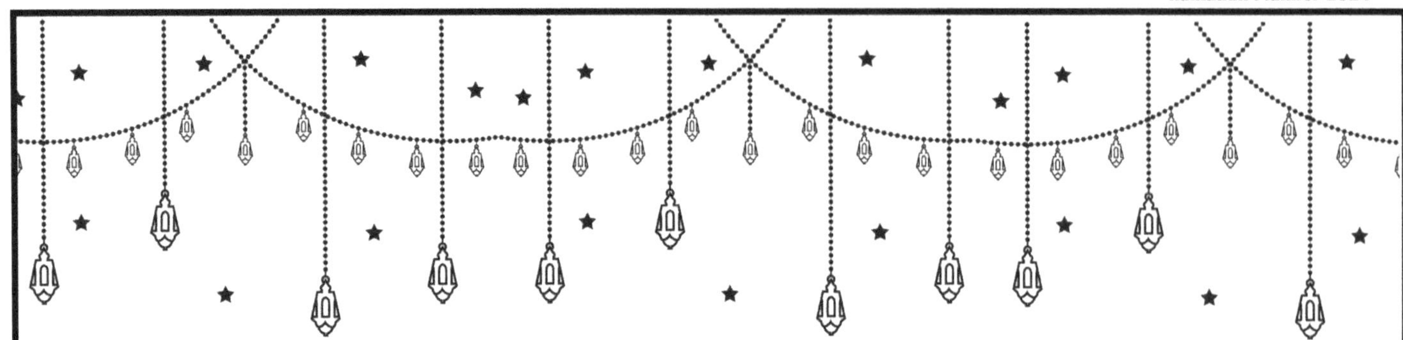

Do you know that the companions of the Prophet Muhammed صلى الله عليه وسلم used to compete with each other in good deeds?

How about you joining the race too with everyone this Ramadan and getting Jannah (Paradise) in reward?

Allah says.."So for this (Paradise) let the competitors compete."   (Al Mutaffifeen, 83:26)

RAMADAN DUAS

رَبَّنَا آتِنَا فِي الدُّنْيَا حَسَنَةً وَفِي الآخِرَةِ حَسَنَةً وَقِنَا عَذَابَ النَّارِ

Our Lord, grant us in the world what is good, and in the Hereafter what is good, and protect us from the punishment of the Fire.(2:201)

رَبَّنَا لَا تُؤَاخِذْنَا إِن نَّسِينَا أَوْ أَخْطَأْنَا

Our Lord! Condemn us not if we forget or fall into error.(2:286)

SPECIAL PRAYERS IN RAMADHAN

2nd Ashra dua' (Days 11-20 of Forgiveness)

اَسْتَغْفِرُ اللهَ رَبِّیْ مِنْ كُلِّ ذَنْبٍ وَّاَتُوْبُ اِلَیْهِ

ASTAGHFIRULLAHA RABBI MIN KULLI
ZAMBIN-WA ATOOBU ILAIHI

I ask forgiveness of my sins from Allah
who is my Lord and I turn towards
Him.

DUA FOR LAYLAT-AL-QADR

Dua for Laylat-Al-Qadr

Hazrat A'isha (r.a.) said, "I said, 'Messenger of Allah, if I know what the night the Night of Power is, what do you think I should say during it?' He said, 'Say:

اللّٰهُمَّ إِنَّكَ عَفُوٌّ تُحِبُّ الْعَفْوَ فَاعْفُ عَنِّي

ALLAHUMMA INNAKA `AFUWWUN
TUHIBBUL `AFWA FA`FU `ANNEE

"O Allah, You are Pardoning and you love pardon, so pardon me."(Tirmidhi)

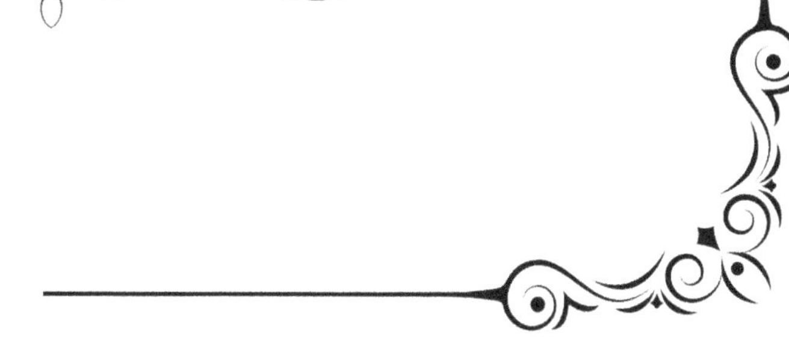

LAYLAT-AL-QADR - THE NIGHT OF POWER

" The Night of Al-Qadr is better than a thousand months. Therein descend the angels and the Rooh [Jibreel (Gabriel)] by Allah's Permission with all Decrees, there is peace until the appearance of dawn." -- Al-Qadar 97:1-5

Ramadan is a special time in Islam, and the last 10 nights are even more important because one of those nights is called Laylat-al-Qadr, or the Night of Power. Allah has made this night really blessed. In the Qur'an, it says,

"We sent it (this Qur'an) down on a blessed night." (Al-Dukhan 44:3)

The Night of Power is the most special night in the Islamic calendar. It's when Angel Jibril revealed the first verses of the Holy Qur'an to Prophet Muhammad. We believe it's on the 27th night of Ramadan, but we're not sure. The Prophet told us to look for it in the last 10 nights of Ramadan, following his example.

He said,

> "Seek Laylat al-Qadr in the last ten days of Ramadan."

Allah values this night more than a thousand months, so it's a chance for us to earn a lot of blessings. It's like a super special night of prayer and devotion.

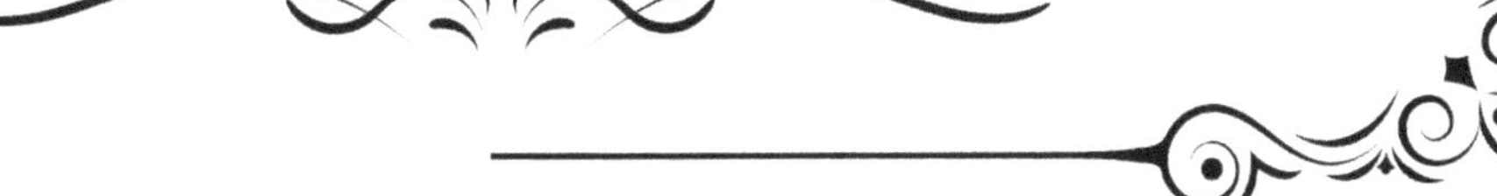

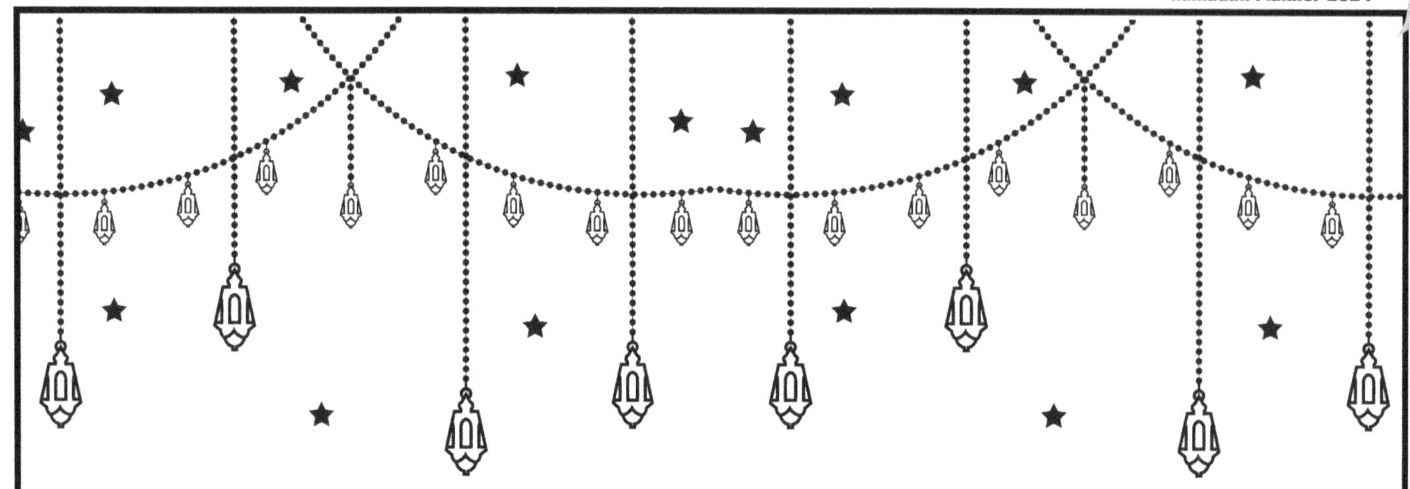

"Happiness will never come to those who fail to appreciate the blessings they already have. Say Alhamdulillah every moment of life"

"Do not lose hope, nor be sad." Quran 3:139

TABLE FOR PRAYER RAKAT

	SUNNAH	FARDH	SUNNAH	NAFL	WITR	NAFL	TOTAL RAKATS
FAJR	2	2	--	--	--	--	4
ZUHR	4	4	2	2			12
ASR	4	4	--	--	--	--	8
MAGHRIB	-	3	2	2	--	--	7
ISHA	4	4	2	2	3	2	17
JUMMAH	4	2	4+2	2	--	--	14

MUAKKADAH   FARDH   WAJIB

Fardh (Farz) - These are mandatory or obligatory prayers. Missing these are a sin on a believer

Sunnah Muakkadah - These are mustahabb (highly encouraged) and the Prophet Muhammad never missed them.

Wajib - This is compulsory but not the same as fardh. Missing is a sin but not the same as fardh.

Nafl - These are optional, Prophet Muhammad occasionally prayed Nafl Salah.

بِسْمِ اللَّهِ الرَّحْمَٰنِ الرَّحِيمِ

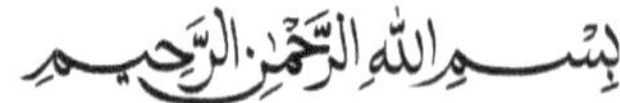

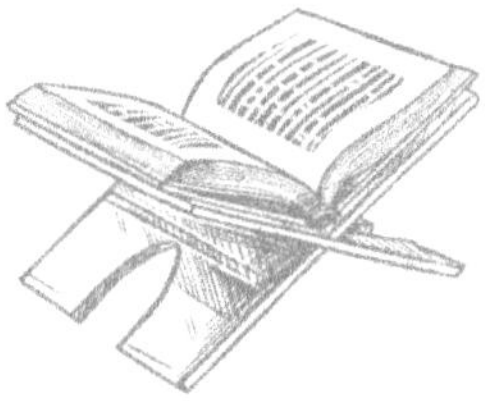

QURAN TRACKER

JUZ 1 ______________________

M	T	W	T	F	S	S

JUZ 2 ______________________

M	T	W	T	F	S	S

JUZ 3 ______________________

M	T	W	T	F	S	S

JUZ 4 ______________________

M	T	W	T	F	S	S

JUZ 5 ______________________

M	T	W	T	F	S	S

JUZ 6 ______________________

M	T	W	T	F	S	S

JUZ 7 ______________________

M	T	W	T	F	S	S

JUZ 8 ______________________

M	T	W	T	F	S	S

JUZ 9 ______________________

M	T	W	T	F	S	S

JUZ 10 ______________________

M	T	W	T	F	S	S

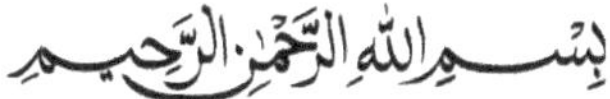

QURAN TRACKER

JUZ 11	M	T	W	T	F	S	S
_______________							

JUZ12	M	T	W	T	F	S	S
_______________							

JUZ 13	M	T	W	T	F	S	S
_______________							

JUZ 14	M	T	W	T	F	S	S
_______________							

JUZ 15	M	T	W	T	F	S	S
_______________							

JUZ 16	M	T	W	T	F	S	S
_______________							

JUZ 17	M	T	W	T	F	S	S
_______________							

JUZ 18	M	T	W	T	F	S	S
_______________							

JUZ 19	M	T	W	T	F	S	S
_______________							

JUZ 20	M	T	W	T	F	S	S
_______________							

بِسْمِ اللهِ الرَّحْمٰنِ الرَّحِيْمِ

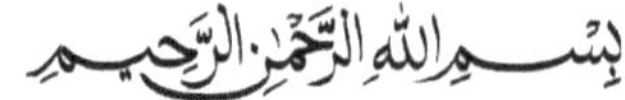

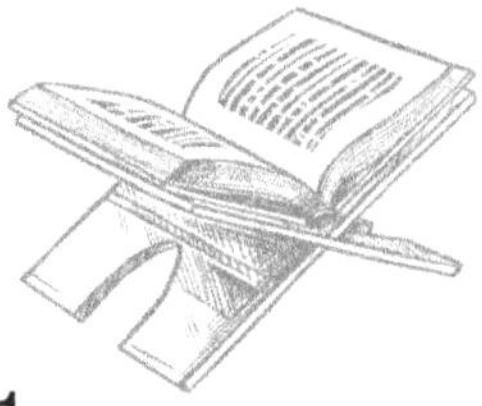

QURAN TRACKER

JUZ 21

M	T	W	T	F	S	S

JUZ 22

M	T	W	T	F	S	S

JUZ 23

M	T	W	T	F	S	S

JUZ 24

M	T	W	T	F	S	S

JUZ 25

M	T	W	T	F	S	S

JUZ 26

M	T	W	T	F	S	S

JUZ 27

M	T	W	T	F	S	S

JUZ 28

M	T	W	T	F	S	S

JUZ 29

M	T	W	T	F	S	S

JUZ 30

M	T	W	T	F	S	S

Alhamdulillah ! Its Eid

TAQABALLAHU MINNA WA MINKUM

May Allah accept (good deeds) from us and from you

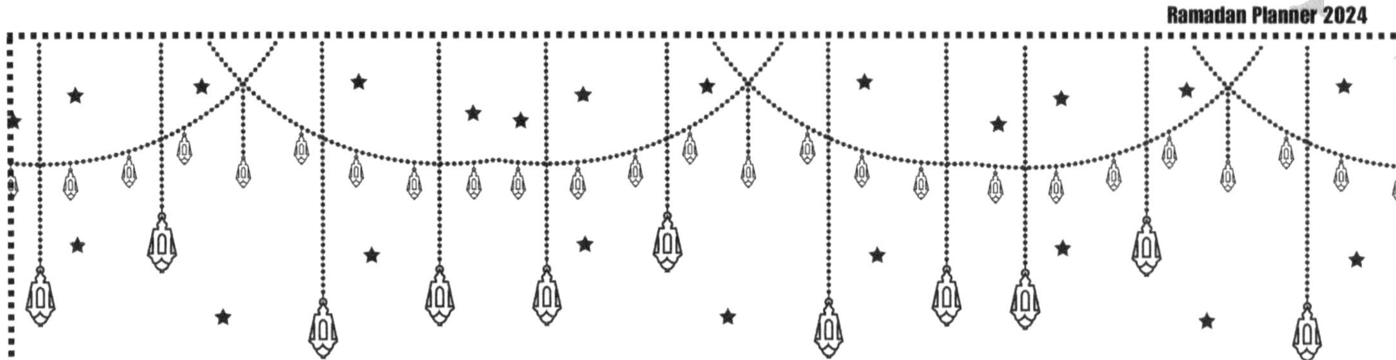

If you found this planner useful, please post a review on this book's Amazon page. Your feedback is valuable for us and will enable us to create better books.

IBADAH CREATIONS

Follow us on social Media:

▶ **Youtube : @ibadahcreations**

⊙ **Instagram: @ibadah_creations**

🌐 **Website: www.surahyaseen.info**

ⓐ **Ibadah Creations**

For further comments please email at: rubyscreations@gmail.com

www.ingramcontent.com/pod-product-compliance
Lightning Source LLC
Chambersburg PA
CBHW040908130726
48005CB00019BA/3017